Flowering Shrubs of Yosemite
and the Sierra Nevada

Flowering Shrubs of
YOSEMITE
and the Sierra Nevada

Watercolors and text by Shirley Spencer

Yosemite Association,   Yosemite, California

Heyday Books, Berkeley, California

Library of Congress Cataloging-in-Publication Data
Spencer, Shirley.
Flowering shrubs of Yosemite and the Sierra Nevada / watercolors and text
by Shirley Spencer.
   p. cm.
 Includes bibliographical references and index.
 ISBN 978-1-59714-112-3 (pbk. : alk. paper)
1. Flowering shrubs—Sierra Nevada (Calif. and Nev.) 2. Flowering
shrubs—California—Yosemite National Park. I. Title.
 SB435.52.C2S64 2008
 582.1709794'4—DC22

            2008023795

Book Design by Rebecca LeGates
Cover images: *Front*, Western Redbud; *back*, Greenleaf Manzanita

This book is the result of a collaboration between the Yosemite Association
and Heyday Books. You can find information about the Yosemite Association
at www.yosemite.org, or write to P.O. Box 230, Yosemite National Park, CA
95318, or call (209) 379-2646. Orders, inquiries, and correspondence about
this book should be addressed to:

        Heyday Books
        P.O. Box 9145, Berkeley, CA 94709
        (510) 549-3564, Fax (510) 549-1889
        www.heydaybooks.com

Printed by Regent in China

10 9 8 7 6 5 4 3 2 1

For my father, William Arthur Haynes, 1928–2002

Contents

Foreword *ix*
Acknowledgments *xi*

White to Cream ◆ *2*

Pink, Purple, and Red ◆ *38*

Orange to Yellow ◆ *56*

Green, Tawny, and Brown ◆ *72*

Glossary *83*
Plant Key *86*
Distribution Areas *87*
References *89*
Indices *90*
Artist's Note *93*
About the Author *95*

Foreword

Malcolm Margolin

VISITORS TO Yosemite National Park and California's Sierra Nevada often arrive with field guides in hand. If interested in plants, they may bring a guide to the wildflowers or perhaps a guide to the trees. These certainly stand them in good stead. But once they settle in and look around, they may find that there is another category of plant that gives the Sierra much of its distinct character—shrubs.

With elevations ranging from 2,000 feet to over 14,000 feet, the Sierra Nevada is blessed with an astonishing variety of flowering shrubs, all interesting, some downright spectacular. Chamise, Mountain Mahogany, Bush Monkeyflower, and Whiteleaf Manzanita are among those that form dense chaparral thickets on dry, hot, low-elevation slopes. American Dogwood, California Rose, and other showy bushes vie for space along streams and in swampy meadows. Still other species of shrubs cling to the rocks in high alpine regions, where long winters and ferocious winds make it impossible for full-sized trees to grow. There they create a rich understory in coniferous forests and clothe otherwise raw road cuts with their tenacious beauty.

While generally underappreciated as a group, shrubs go a long way toward defining the Sierra experience. The arrival of spring here is announced boldly to all by the Western Redbud, as "pea-shaped flowers thickly cover the naked branches, giving the impression of a pink cloud of color from afar." The dominant experience that hikers bring back from walks through coniferous forests is not only the image of trees but the memory of the musky odors that suffuse the hot summer air, a rich reservoir of scent created by understory shrubs.

Shirley Spencer's *Flowering Shrubs of Yosemite and the Sierra Nevada* presents a selection of forty plants. They range from those with conspicuous, showy flowers such as the Flannelbush, the Bush Poppy, and the American Dogwood to the more humble.

While this book, with its graceful and meticulously rendered watercolors and precise botanical descriptions, will serve as a field guide, it offers something more—an invitation to see the world afresh through the eyes of a skilled artist and passionate observer. Many Californians are familiar with the Toyon bush, or Christmas Berry, whose red berries brighten the state's drab winter landscape. How many have looked closely enough, however, to realize that these berries "are not perfectly round; they have irregularly puckered ends"?

And other senses are evoked as well as the visual. After describing Mountain Misery, Spencer invites us to press a leaf between the fingers so that "tiny glands will release a scent and leave a sticky residue on the skin." Am I the only one who didn't realize that the berry of the Blue Elderberry only appears to be blue; if the ripe fruit is rubbed gently "it proves to be black underneath a powdery whitish coating." Even the sense of hearing is called into play, as Spencer describes how the seed pod of the Bush Lupine "explodes with an audible pop [as] the tan mottled seeds are expelled a remarkable distance from the parent shrub."

More than just a field guide, *Flowering Shrubs of Yosemite and the Sierra Nevada* pays loving homage to beauty and diversity, presented as a gift and an offering by a careful observer and a consummately accomplished artist. It is one of those rare books that can be taken into the field or placed on a coffee table with equal pleasure. It is a book not just to use but to cherish.

Acknowledgments

THANK YOU TO the staff and faculty of Fresno Pacific University for support and encouragement throughout the compilation and completion of this text. Specific thanks to Dave Youngs for his belief in me and this project, to Richard Wiebe for encouragement of my writing skills, and to Rod Janzen for understanding the initial vision of what I wanted to accomplish. An enormous thank you to Doug Hansen, art professor at Fresno State University, who added tremendously to my knowledge and ability as an artist; thank you for your inspiration and for encouraging me to believe in my work.

There were many people who were instrumental in providing access to dried herbarium sheets, fresh botanical specimens, native shrubs, and high-quality photos of some of the plants in flower or fruit, and who willingly allowed me to observe, sketch, and work off of the materials. A grateful thank you to Madeline Burton, Donna Lalev, Michelle Lalev, and Roger S. Reid, staff and participant of the Episcopalian Conference Center of Oakhurst, all of whom provided materials and photos integral to the making of this book. Appreciation is due also to Michael Kunz of Fresno Pacific University, who advised me on which shrubs to include in the book, along with graciously providing me with some of his excellent photography for reference during the artistic process. Thank you to Bonnie Bladen of Intermountain Nursery, who provided me with insight and photographs that helped in the selection and painting of the artwork in this book, and to Joanna Clines, United States

Forest Service Botanist, who gave me access to native Sierra Nevada shrub photography. A huge thanks goes to Somer Burrough of the Bureau of Land Management for her knowledge and sharing of information regarding the use of plant materials by Native Americans. I wish to express appreciation to Dave Woolley of the Bureau of Reclamation for access to the Friant Water Education Garden to observe native shrubs.

The staff at the Yosemite Association was and is key in the completion of this process. I wish to express my appreciation to Pete Devine, Education Director, for giving me the idea to write and illustrate a shrub guidebook to the Sierra Nevada. A gracious thanks to the late Steve Medley, former Executive Director, for his patience and belief in my ability to complete this project, and also to the board members of the Yosemite Association for agreeing to publish the completed work.

An expression of appreciation is due to my personal friends and family, who have unfailingly given support and encouragement during this process. I wish to thank Beth Linder for her expert editing of the initial drafts of all the text. Love and appreciation to Anita Goetz, Jeannine Koshear, Val Messervy, and Wendy Stevens for their firsthand experience and advice on the academic process. Thank you to Ann Neal of Auberry Library for encouragement and listening skills. A heartfelt thank you to my mother, Joyce Haynes-Palaio, and my stepfather, Ted Palaio, for their love and unwavering belief in me.

And, finally, I am grateful to my beloved husband, Mark Spencer, the one who offered love, support, encouragement, patience, and computer savvy throughout the entire process. This book is dedicated to you, Mark, love of my life; without you, this project would have been impossible.

Flowering Shrubs of
YOSEMITE
and the Sierra Nevada

Blue Elderberry

Sambucus mexicana

Botanical Family: Caprifoliaceae
Elevation: Below 9,800 ft. (3000 m)
Plant Community Zone: Sierra Nevada Foothills, Lower and Upper
  Montane
Shrub Height: 7–26 ft. (2–8 m)
Flower: Tiny, numerous, and white or cream-colored
Fruit: Small, round, black or blue berries
Distribution: Open forests and riparian habitat

The Sierra Nevada is host to the deciduous Blue Elderberry, also
called the Mexican Elderberry. At maturity, the older branches
present an open, sparse look, with the new growth coming in dense
and dark green. Leaves of the Blue Elderberry are serrate and have
a pinnate arrangement along their stems. The leaf base is often
asymmetrical; the blade on one side of the midvein sometimes joins
the stem at a slightly higher point on the blade than it does on the
other side. Tiny white or cream flowers cluster at the top of uplifted
stems, and as the flowers develop, their weight can sometimes cause
the young stems to droop. On close inspection, one can make out
five calyxes and five corollas, with stamens alternating between the
petals. Late summer and autumn bring dense groupings of hanging
berries on the shrub. At first glance the ripe fruit appears to be light
blue, but if it is rubbed gently, it proves to be black underneath a
powdery whitish coating. Blue Elderberry is commonly found in
open forests or riparian habitats of the Sierra, and smaller species
of Elderberry can be found at even higher elevations. In certain
environments, several different species can be found together.
Some Native American peoples hollow out the pith of the Blue
Elderberry stem for use as a percussion instrument, and other local
people collect the ripe berries and prepare wine or jam from the tart
fruit. Raw Blue Elderberry should not be consumed in large quanti-
ties as it is toxic.

American Dogwood
Cornus sericea

Botanical Family: Cornaceae
Elevation: Below 9,200 ft. (2800 m)
Plant Community Zone: Sierra Nevada Foothills, Lower and Upper
   Montane, Subalpine
Shrub Height: 5–13 ft. (1.5–4 m)
Flower: Numerous, white, and arranged in loose clusters
Fruit: White or cream-colored furrowed drupes
Distribution: Wet meadows, riparian areas, and moist forests

The most well-known Dogwood in the Sierra Nevada is the tree-sized Mountain Dogwood—showy in spring and with pinkish leaves that light up the coniferous forest in autumn—but the lesser-known American Dogwood can be just as attractive, especially in winter, when the smooth, bright red, upright stems of this deciduous shrub are silhouetted against the pure white of the first snowfall. Under the younger stems of this many-branched shrub is older, gray wood growing close to the ground. The leaves are dark green on their tops, with the bottom leaf surfaces exhibiting a lighter green and protruding veins. Many minute white flowers are clustered atop light green stems, and flower parts are generally in groups of four: four sepals, four petals, and four stamens, with the stamens and single pistil extending well beyond the other flower parts. The fruits are white to cream-colored and furrowed on the sides; the terms "drupe" and "stone fruit" are used to describe these and other fleshy fruits with thin outer skins and a single hard seed within. (Other examples are cherries and apricots). American Dogwood thrives in many moist habitats, including riparian areas, wet meadows, and lake edges.

Pinemat Manzanita
Arctostaphylos nevadensis

Botanical Family: Ericaceae
Elevation: 3,000–9,800 ft. (900–3000 m)
Plant Community Zone: Lower and Upper Montane, Subalpine
Shrub Height: Up to 2 ft. (60 cm)
Flower: Small, white or light pink, and urn-shaped
Fruit: Round, brownish, and berry-like
Distribution: Rocky slopes and open coniferous forests

At the higher elevations of the Sierra Nevada, one may encounter the Pinemat Manzanita spreading over granite and forest soils. This prostrate evergreen shrub is conspicuous in coniferous forests with its smooth and shiny reddish brown stems creeping along the ground. Pinemat Manzanita can be found spread out like a mat but also mounded up in a clump. The small, bright green leaves are smooth on the edges, approximately the same color on both sides, and are held upright above the stems. The small, unobtrusive urn-shaped flower is white with a hint of pink around the top and bottom. The flowers are arranged in small clusters on the ends of the twigs. If pollinated, the flowers produce fruit in late summer and autumn, and the round, brownish berries grow in attractive bunches, each fruit looking somewhat like a "little apple," which is a translation of the Spanish-origin word "manzanita." The fruits of Pinemat Manzanita are highly desirable to many Sierra Nevada animals for autumn feeding. Pinemat Manzanita is found in thin granite soils, high-elevation coniferous forests, and on rocky slopes.

Greenleaf Manzanita
Arctostaphylos patula

Botanical Family: Ericaceae
Elevation: 2,500–11,000 ft. (750–3350 m)
Plant Community Zone: Lower and Upper Montane, Subalpine,
    Alpine
Shrub Height: 3–7 ft. (1–2 m)
Flower: Pinkish white, urn-shaped, and clustered
Fruit: Round, smooth, and dark brown
Distribution: Open coniferous forest and exposed slopes

Greenleaf Manzanita branches are smooth and reddish brown, and
the paper-thin bark peels off in strips. Younger stems are a lighter
shade of green-brown. The twigs have glands that, when seen
through a hand lens, look glossy and golden. Some Greenleaf Manzanita may have lower branches rooting on the ground. The shiny,
oval, green leaves are smooth, and the edges are entire. Pinkish
white flowers are urn-shaped, with reflexed petal lobes surrounding the small opening. In autumn, the smooth, round fruit of the
Greenleaf Manzanita is reddish brown and resembles a miniature
apple, which gave the shrub its name: "manzanita" is a word of
Spanish origin that means "little apple." This Manzanita is found in
open coniferous forests within a wide range of habitats, and wildlife
depend on its fruit as an integral part of their autumn diet.

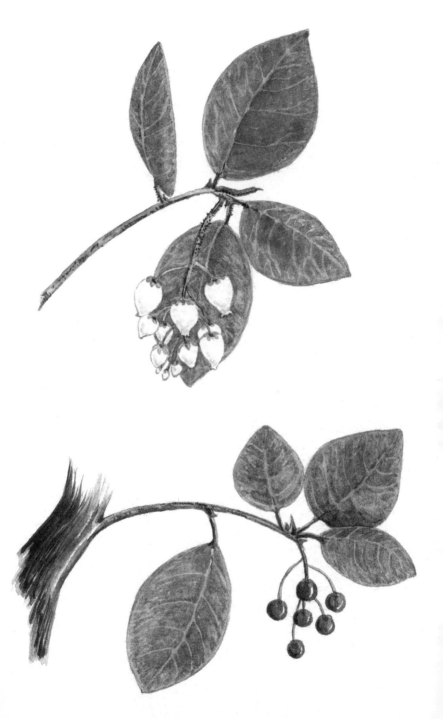

Whiteleaf Manzanita
Arctostaphylos viscida

Botanical Family: Ericaceae
Elevation: 500–6,100 ft. (150–1850 m)
Plant Community Zone: Sierra Nevada Foothills, Lower Montane
Shrub Height: 3–16+ ft. (1–5+ m)
Flower: White or pinkish and urn-shaped
Fruit: Smooth and reddish brown
Distribution: Oak woodlands, chaparral, and dry coniferous forests

Whiteleaf Manzanita is a large upright shrub found in many habitats of the Sierra Nevada. Under favorable circumstances, the primary branches of the shrub can be quite large in diameter, giving it the appearance of a small multi-branched tree. Whiteleaf Manzanita bark is smooth and dark red-brown and will peel in thin strips to allow for expansion as the trunk grows in circumference. Smaller twigs and petioles can be glandular and hairy and, if pressed between the fingers, can leave a sticky residue. The oval leaves have smooth margins, and their distinctive coloration is gray-green with a glaucous white powder-like coating. White to pinkish, urn-shaped spring flowers are clustered near the tips of the branches. Autumn fruit is sticky, spherical, and reddish brown, hanging in tight groups quite conspicuous against the lighter gray-green leaves, and both mammals and birds depend on the nutritious fruits for autumn fare. Whiteleaf Manzanita is found in oak woodland communities, dry coniferous forests, and on open chaparral slopes. Landowners in the Sierra Nevada who find Whiteleaf Manzanita growing naturally on their property will often shape and prune up the lower branches of this shrub to enjoy its beauty and drought-tolerant qualities.

White Heather
Cassiope mertensiana

Botanical Family: Ericaceae
Elevation: 5,900–11,500 ft. (1800–3500 m)
Plant Community Zone: Lower and Upper Montane, Subalpine,
　Alpine
Shrub Height: Up to 1 ft. (30 cm)
Flower: Fused, white, and bell-shaped; subtended by red sepals and
　stems
Fruit: Chambered capsule
Distribution: Moist subalpine meadows and wet rocky slopes

White Heather, found in high-elevation meadows of the Sierra
Nevada, can be an elusive shrub, but one well worth searching
for. This small, prostrate shrub has many branches that may root
and trail along granite boulders and rocky soils. The small, leathery, elliptic evergreen leaves are compressed against the stems,
and looking closely at their edges one can see that they are either
smooth or, more infrequently, lined with minute hairs on their
margins. The most dramatic feature of White Heather is its flowers, which blossom in an abundant swath of color. Many fused,
white, bell-shaped flowers hang individually from deep red sepals
and arching stems, providing a dramatic contrast in color. The
fused petals that flare back at the flower opening typically have five
lobes. The fruit is a chambered capsule, with several seeds in each
chamber. White Heather is found in moist subalpine meadows and
tucked among granite outcroppings that receive moisture from late
snowdrifts. Eminent naturalist John Muir was known to extol the
charm of the White Heather: "Here too…I met Cassiope [White
Heather] growing in fringes among the battered rocks. No evangel
among all the mountain plants speaks Nature's love more plainly
than Cassiope."

Western Azalea
Rhododendron occidentale

Botanical Family: Ericaceae
Elevation: Below 7,200 ft. (2200 m)
Plant Community Zone: Sierra Nevada Foothills, Lower and Upper
  Montane
Shrub Height: 2–10 ft. (60 cm–3 m)
Flower: Fragrant, white with yellow blotches on the upper petal,
  and elongated stamens
Fruit: Capsule; dehiscent tip to base
Distribution: Riparian areas and coniferous forests

Spring is the showy season for the Western Azalea. The new, light
green leaves of this deciduous shrub grow on the dense brownish branches in an alternating pattern. The leaf's shape is elliptic,
and minute hairs grow along the edges. Shortly after leafing out,
atop the stems bloom clumps of flowers: white with an upper petal
marked by yellow splotches of color, and with the stamens and pistil extending far beyond the petals. Their fragrance can be smelled
from afar on summer days, and the nectar in the funnel-shaped
flowers is sweet. After pollination, fruit appears subsequent to the
petals dropping off, leaving a green chambered capsule with many
seeds per chamber. Western Azalea is found thriving in vast stands
in moist environments. It will clump around seeps or springs as
well. In some Giant Sequoia groves, the Western Azalea can be
found blooming sweetly along riparian habitat.

Huckleberry Oak
Quercus vaccinifolia

Botanical Family: Fagaceae
Elevation: 3,000–9,200 ft. (900–2800 m)
Plant Community Zone: Sierra Nevada Foothills, Lower and Upper
    Montane, Subalpine
Shrub Height: Up to 5 ft. (1.5 m)
Flower: Tiny, short-stalked, and located in upper leaves
Fruit: Small, round acorn topped by thin, flat scales
Distribution: Rocky ridges and coniferous and subalpine forests

In coniferous forests, one may encounter the prostrate evergreen form of the Huckleberry Oak. If the shrub exhibits no flowers or fruit, one might be unsure about its identity. Most other oaks are massive and upright, in contrast to the Huckleberry Oak, whose smooth, gray, woody stems spread low to the ground. The small evergreen leaves are oblong with a pointed tip, and the edges are mostly smooth but can display an occasional serration. The leaves are a uniform green color, with new twigs and leaves sprouting a lighter pale green. The small staminate and pistillate flowers are located in the upper leaves of the Huckleberry Oak. The most recognizable part of any oak is the fruit that most people identify as an acorn. The acorn of the Huckleberry Oak is small and round and takes two years to mature. Acorns are a vital food source for many animals of the Sierra Nevada, and early Native populations also relied on the fruit of various oak trees as an integral part of their diet. This shrub is found in coniferous forests, on rocky ridges and slopes, and extending up into subalpine forests.

California Buckeye
Aesculus californica

Botanical Family: Hippocastanaceae
Elevation: Below 5,600 ft. (1700 m)
Plant Community Zone: Sierra Nevada Foothills, Lower Montane
Shrub Height: 13–39 ft. (4–12 m)
Flower: Numerous, showy, white to pinkish, and clustered along an
upright stem
Fruit: Leathery skin encasing a smooth, round, brown seed
Distribution: Dry slopes, open woodlands, and riparian areas

California Buckeye is a large shrub or small tree found primarily
in the lower elevations of the Sierra Nevada. Large, bright green,
glossy leaves are finely serrated on the edges and grow in a palmate
configuration. California Buckeye is one of the first and most dramatic shrubs to leaf out in the spring. It is, however, summer deciduous—its leaves curl up and turn brown on the stems in mid-summer
in response to long, hot, dry weather in the foothill regions of the
Sierra Nevada. Many small white flowers cluster thickly along a
green stem, making for a dramatic display in spring. The unpleas-
antly scented flowers are asymmetrical, with numerous elongated
stamens tipped with orange pollen. In mid-summer, as the leaves
dry up, large leathery fruits hang from bare stems. The thick, fleshy
covering of the fruit peels off to reveal a hard spherical seed. Brown
and glossy, the seeds root in the soft, wet soil of winter on the
woodland forest floor. All parts of the California Buckeye are toxic
to humans when raw. This interesting shrub is located in canyons,
open woodlands, riparian areas, and on dry slopes.

Tree Anemone
Carpenteria californica

Botanical Family: Philadelphaceae
Elevation: 1,500–3,300 ft. (450–1000 m)
Plant Community Zone: Sierra Nevada Foothills, Lower Montane
Shrub Height: Up to 10 ft. (3 m)
Flower: Large, white, fragrant, and with numerous yellow stamens
Fruit: Green, spherical, growing atop exposed stems
Distribution: Streambanks and cool oak woodlands

The rare Tree Anemone has dark green, leathery leaves that grow opposite each other on the branch. In many cases, the outer edge of the leaf is rolled under itself. Gray, peeling bark and dark green leaves provide a striking contrast to the spring flowers. Each fragrant white bloom exhibits a large, green, fleshy superior ovary surrounded by numerous yellow stamens, and can grow as large as two inches across. The summer fruit is a round, greenish tan knob held atop the stems. The Tree Anemone's native habitat is confined to the foothills between the San Joaquin River and the Kings River watersheds. During the dry, hot summers, some leaves turn yellow and drop off the lower branches, giving the shrub a distressed appearance. Once the cool and moist days of spring return, however, stems begin to grow new, lush growth. Tree Anemone is known to be fire-resistant and has been observed to "root-sprout" after a fire. If the habitat is conducive, the Tree Anemone can also be cultivated in the home garden; *Carpenteria californica* is increasingly popular with homeowners who desire a unique and uncommon shrub. Several organizations in eastern Fresno County offer springtime hikes to see these magnificent flowering shrubs in their native habitat.

Mock Orange
Philadelphus lewisii

Botanical Family: Philadelphaceae
Elevation: Below 4,900 ft. (1500 m)
Plant Community Zone: Sierra Nevada Foothills, Lower Montane
Shrub Height: Up to 10 ft. (3 m)
Flower: Showy, fragrant, white, and with numerous stamens
Fruit: Elongated, dehiscent capsule with numerous seeds
Distribution: Open forest and woodland, and exposed slopes and
   canyons

It is a memorable experience to come upon a Mock Orange in full
bloom. Older, woody stems of this impressive shrub are gray in
color, while the younger twigs are green or light reddish brown.
The green leaf blade is ovate, or egg-shaped, and has three prominent veins originating at the base. Leaf margins are mostly smooth,
although there is an occasional toothed edge. The inflorescence, or
grouping of flowers, has the qualities of a raceme: flowers aligned
along the branch on small stems that bloom sequentially from bottom to top. In some cases, however, the terminal or top bud will
blossom first. Four white petals encircle numerous yellow stamens
arranged around an ovary that is branched at the tip. Occasionally
a petal may have a small notch at the end. Mock Orange flowers are
unmistakably fragrant. The fruit is a woody capsule with abundant
seeds. Mock Orange is not a common shrub, but it is one worth
seeking due to the beauty and fragrance of its flowers. Its favored
environments are cooler canyons and slopes, riparian areas, and
open woodlands.

Mountain Whitethorn
Ceanothus cordulatus

Botanical Family: Rhamnaceae
Elevation: 3,000–9,500 ft. (900–2900 m)
Plant Community Zone: Sierra Nevada Foothills, Lower and Upper
    Montane, Subalpine
Shrub Height: Up to 5 ft. (1.5 m)
Flower: Tiny, white to cream-colored, and growing in an elongated
    cluster
Fruit: Green, three-lobed capsule tinted with red
Distribution: Coniferous forests, exposed ridges, and rocky slopes

Mountain Whitethorn is a common member of the genus *Ceano-thus*. It is a dense, spreading shrub with light gray-green branches. Arranged along the stems are long, sharp thorns that may protrude past the alternate evergreen leaves, which are elliptic and have three dominant veins that originate from the leaf base. Mountain Whitethorn has a smaller overall leaf size than the similar Deer Brush, and the leaves are grayish green, with the upper surface darker than the lower surface. The upper side of the leaf occasionally demonstrates a concave appearance along the central leaf vein. Elongated clusters of tiny white to cream-colored flowers are arranged along the terminal branches. Upon close inspection, one can see that each minute flower has at its center a green ovary surrounded by white or cream-colored flower parts, and long extruded stamens located opposite the petals. The fruit is a green, three-lobed capsule tinted with red. Mountain Whitethorn is found atop exposed ridges, throughout coniferous forests, in open woodlands, and often in the drier areas of the many Giant Sequoia groves of the Sierra Nevada.

Deer Brush
Ceanothus integerrimus

Botanical Family: Rhamnaceae
Elevation: 1,000–6,900 ft. (300–2100 m)
Plant Community Zone: Sierra Nevada Foothills, Lower and Upper
   Montane
Shrub Height: Up to 13 ft. (4 m)
Flower: Dense, small, white to cream-colored, and arranged along
   upright stems
Fruit: Sticky, three-lobed capsule
Distribution: Coniferous forests and open slopes

There are many species of *Ceanothus* in the state of California,
and a number are specific to the Sierra Nevada. The growth pattern of Deer Brush is up and out and is less dense than the similar
Whitethorn. The stems are green and smooth and, unlike many
other species of the *Ceanothus* genus, Deer Brush stems don't have
thorns. Elliptic leaves with smooth margins have three obvious
veins branching out from the leaf base. The lush foliage is deciduous in autumn, exposing bare branches through the winter months.
Numerous small flowers are clustered in a spike at the end of each
branch. The flowers can be white or cream and sometimes have
a slight blue tint. The fruit is a sticky, round capsule with three
valves. Deer Brush is found on sunny slopes and dry ridges, and
Ceanothus as a group is generally drought-tolerant and adapted to
fire. Many shrubs within this genus are prone to hybridization; there
may be some variation in individual plants.

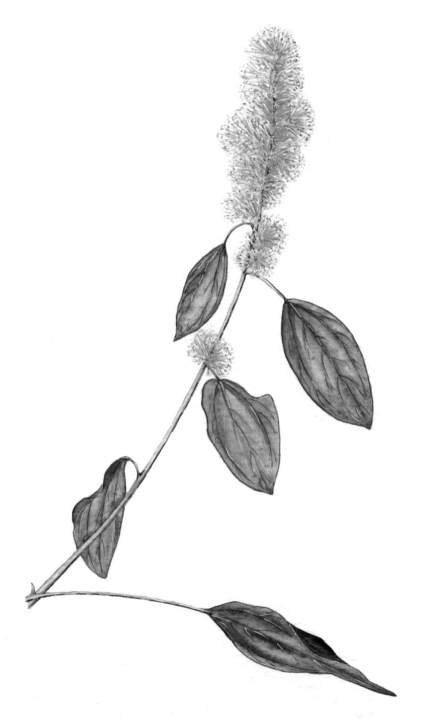

Chamise
Adenostoma fasciculatum

Botanical Family: Rosaceae
Elevation: Below 5,300 ft. (1600 m)
Plant Community Zone: Sierra Nevada Foothills, Lower Montane
Shrub Height: Up to 13 ft. (4 m)
Flower: Small, white to cream-colored, and clustered as a spike on stem ends
Fruit: Dry achene
Distribution: Arid ridges, exposed slopes, rocky canyons, and chaparral

Chamise is a dominant member of the chaparral plant community and can be found in nearly pure stands in arid settings of the Sierra Nevada. This shrub is multi-branched and grows stiffly upright. The grayish brown bark has a rough texture; on older woody stems, it can be smooth or slightly hairy, and peeling. Small, evergreen, needle-like leaves are clustered in groups along the stems. All herbaceous parts of Chamise are resinous and, if pressed gently between the fingers, will leave a sticky, aromatic residue. Small white or cream-colored flowers cluster along yellowish green terminal stems. The flowers are numerous and densely packed and, when in full bloom, appear as concentrated plumes at the ends of the branches. Upon close inspection of the flower, it is easy to see five petals with many yellow stamens grouped alternately between the petals. The fruit is a typical achene—dry and encasing one seed. Chamise is found inhabiting dry ridges, open slopes, rocky canyons, and chaparral communities. The shrub is flammable and can contribute to the intensity of wildfires.

Mountain Misery
Chamaebatia foliolosa

Botanical Family: Rosaceae
Elevation: 2,000–7,200 ft. (600–2200 m)
Plant Community Zone: Sierra Nevada Foothills, Lower and Upper
   Montane
Shrub Height: 1–2 ft. (30–60 cm)
Flower: Five bright white petals surround numerous yellow stamens
Fruit: Round, brown achenes clustered atop stems
Distribution: Open coniferous forests and exposed slopes

Mountain Misery is a dense groundcover found extensively in some
forests of the Sierra Nevada. The woody stems are grayish brown,
with alternating evergreen leaves. The leaf arrangement of Mountain Misery is pinnate, or feather-like; along the central leaf vein
are smaller leaflets, each of which is itself twice divided into even
smaller sections. On warm summer days, vast slopes of Mountain
Misery emit a strong musky odor into the atmosphere. If the leaf
is pressed between the fingers, tiny glands will release a scent and
leave a sticky residue on the skin. Some people claim to enjoy
the strong smell of this shrub, although most consider it a nega-
tive odor. Looking closely, one will notice minute glandular hairs
covering the younger stems. White flowers with five round petals
and abundant yellow stamens adorn this shrub in early summer.
The fruit is a brown achene that emerges in mid-summer at lower
elevations and late summer at higher elevations. Mountain Misery
spreads as groundcover in open coniferous forests. After a forest
fire, this shrub has the ability to, quickly and vigorously, sprout new
leaves from the roots of the blackened plant.

Toyon
Heteromeles arbutifolia

Botanical Family: Rosaceae
Elevation: Below 4,300 ft. (1300 m)
Plant Community Zone: Sierra Nevada Foothills, Lower Montane
Shrub Height: Up to 16 ft. (5 m)
Flower: Five white petals surround many paired yellow stamens
Fruit: Bright red, fleshy but dry berry, with an irregular shape
Distribution: Coniferous forests, open woodlands, and chaparral

Toyon, or Christmas Berry, as it is sometimes called, is a large shrub suited to many environments in the Sierra Nevada. The many-branched trunk is grayish in color, but it is nearly covered by large, leathery evergreen leaves. Young stems are a reddish brown color. Upper surfaces of the leaves are dark green, while the lower surfaces are paler. Leaf margins are deeply toothed. At the ends of the branches are numerous small flowers, each with five white petals cupped around many paired yellow stamens. Perhaps the most interesting part of Toyon is the shiny, bright red berries massed together on the reddish stems during the autumn and winter months. Toyon fruits are not perfectly round; they have irregularly puckered ends. Birds utilize the dry, mealy fruits for food during winter months. Toyon can be found in many habitats, including open woodlands, chaparral communities, and coniferous forests. Due to its interesting winter color, Toyon is used frequently in drought-tolerant or xeric gardens throughout California.

Bitter Cherry
Prunus emarginata

Botanical Family: Rosaceae
Elevation: Below 9,200 ft. (2800 m)
Plant Community Zone: Sierra Nevada Foothills, Lower and Upper
  Montane, Subalpine
Shrub Height: 3–33 ft. (1–10 m)
Flower: White flowers with numerous protruding stamens
Fruit: Red, pulpy, shiny, and encasing a small, hard seed
Distribution: Open woodlands, coniferous forests, and canyons

Bitter Cherry can be a large shrub or a small tree. Older branches
and stems are smooth, with mottled reddish gray bark. Young stems
are reddish green, with the leaves grouped on small auxiliary stems,
alternately spaced loosely along the branches. The deciduous leaves
are elliptic, with fine-toothed serrations along the margins. Young
leaves have a reddish tint to their edges. Five white petals unfold
above light green sepals, and elongated white stamens tipped with
yellow anthers extend conspicuously around the centered pistil.
After the flower is pollinated, shiny, red, round fruits hang on
the branches in late summer and autumn. The flesh of the Bitter
Cherry fruit is pulpy and conceals a hard, stone-like seed within.
Fruits of the Bitter Cherry are an important food source for certain bird species, but they are usually much too bitter for modern
humans. This widespread shrub has adapted to a variety of climatic
conditions and can be found thriving densely in canyons or forests
and growing sparsely in chaparral communities and on open slopes.

Thimbleberry
Rubus parviflorus

Botanical Family: Rosaceae
Elevation: Below 8,200 ft. (2500 m)
Plant Community Zone: Sierra Nevada Foothills, Lower and Upper
  Montane
Shrub Height: Up to 10 ft. (3 m)
Flower: Showy, white, and with numerous center stamens
Fruit: Red, round, fleshy, aggregate, and edible
Distribution: Shady coniferous forests and moist woodlands

Thimbleberry is an upward-growing, deciduous shrub with large, velvet-like leaves. Unlike most members of the *Rosaceae* family, it has smooth branches and stems that are devoid of thorns or prickles. The simple leaves have an obvious five-lobed shape that resembles a maple leaf. Small teeth on the leaf margins accentuate the palmate shape of the leaf. Above the soft leaves, thin, green stems covered with tiny glands support white flowers. Five green sepals and five white petals surround the numerous yellow stamens and few pistils. In late summer and early autumn, the Thimbleberry bears edible raspberry-like fruit; it is ruby red and separates completely from the receptacle when picked. The "berry" of the Thimbleberry is actually a tight, round cluster of many fleshy, sweet achenes. They are highly desirable to wildlife. Native Thimbleberry is found in the shade of coniferous forests and in cool, moist woodlands.

Spicebush
Calycanthus occidentalis

Botanical Family: Calycanthaceae
Elevation: Below 4,900 ft. (1500 m)
Plant Community Zone: Sierra Nevada Foothills, Lower Montane
Shrub Height: 3–10+ ft. (1–3+ m)
Flower: Large, showy, crimson-colored, and with strap-like petals
Fruit: Leathery achene
Distribution: Riparian areas, woodlands, and cool, shady, moist
    forests

Spicebush is a wonderful shrub to behold in spring or summer, both
with the eyes and with the nose. This deciduous shrub has woody
perennial stems, and the new spring growth of twigs is supple and
light green. Large chartreuse-colored leaves are smooth on the edge
and located opposite each other on the branch. When the leaves
are crushed or rubbed between the fingers, they release a strong
citrus odor that is reminiscent of grapefruit rind. The buds of the
flowers are held atop the ends of the stems, and when they bloom,
Spicebush flowers are large and showy. The many deep crimson petals are strap-like, and the closer they get to the center of the flower,
the shorter and more curled they are. Hidden deep in the throat
of the flower are numerous stamens. In late summer and autumn,
as the leaves turn a yellowish brown, the fruit—a large, ovoid,
leathery achene—is easily visible at the tips of the branches. The
seeds shake out easily from the hollow receptacle. Spicebush prefers
cool and moist conditions in shady canyons or riparian areas. This
dramatic shrub has also been planted in many gardens as an ornamental and, if given supplemental water, can grow in areas that are
unlike its natural habitat.

Snowberry
Symphoricarpos albus

Botanical Family: Caprifoliaceae
Elevation: Below 3,900 ft. (1200 m)
Plant Community Zone: Sierra Nevada Foothills, Lower Montane
Shrub Height: 2–6 ft. (60 cm–2 m)
Flower: Small, white or pink, and bell-shaped
Fruit: Round, white berries
Distribution: Shady woodlands, riparian areas, and moist canyons

Snowberry is a small, erect deciduous shrub that, without its blossoms or berries, might be overlooked on the forest floor. Older stems are brown, and younger stems are bright green. The leaf is simple, oval, and smooth on the edge, with a short petiole attaching it to the stem. Snowberry leaves are arranged opposite each other along the stem. The small white or pink flowers are bell-shaped and grouped in upright clusters. The petals are fused together at the base, and only at the tip do they separate into five small, flaring lobes. In autumn, the colors of the forest and the yellowish leaves of the Snowberry contrast against the mature white berries clumped along the branch. Many white berries are toxic to humans, and Snowberry itself is considered inedible. Preferred habitats for this delicate Sierra Nevada shrub are moist canyons, shady woodlands, and riparian areas.

Mountain Heather
Phyllodoce breweri

Botanical Family: Ericaceae
Elevation: 3,900–11,500 ft. (1200–3500 m)
Plant Community Zone: Lower and Upper Montane, Subalpine,
    Alpine
Shrub Height: 4–12 in. (10–30 cm)
Flower: Deep pink, with a flaring cup shape and elongated stamens
Fruit: Chambered capsule with winged seeds
Distribution: Subalpine meadows, shady forests, and damp slopes

Mountain Heather is a matted, prostrate shrub found in the upper
elevations of the Sierra Nevada, sometimes in the same habitat
as White Heather. Older twigs are gray and textured, while the
younger stems are green, with numerous small, stiff, linear leaves
surrounding the stem. The needle-like leaves are dark green and,
to some extent, resemble those of a coniferous evergreen tree.
Mountain Heather has small, deep-pink blossoms shaped like flared
cups that sit in clusters at the ends of the stems. The most obvious feature of the flower is the showy stamens and lengthy pistil
that extend beyond the edge of the bloom. In late summer and
early autumn, the fruits, chambered capsules that contain slightly
winged seeds, appear atop the stems. The preferred environment of
the Mountain Heather is moist subalpine meadows, shady coniferous forests, lakeshores, and wet rocky slopes. A companion plant
of the Mountain Heather, the Alpine Laurel, *Kalmia polifolia,* has a
similar-looking flower at first glance, but upon closer inspection the
foliage of the two shrubs is vastly different; the Alpine Laurel has
regular, oblong leaves with smooth edges instead of the needle-like
leaves of the Mountain Heather.

Western Redbud
Cercis occidentalis

Botanical Family: Fabaceae
Elevation: 300–4,900 ft. (90–1500 m)
Plant Community Zone: Sierra Nevada Foothills, Lower Montane
Shrub Height: Up to 23 ft. (7 m)
Flower: Small, numerous, and pink
Fruit: Flat, oblong, brown dehiscent pods
Distribution: Open, dry slopes and canyons, and streamsides and
　　ravines

Blooming Western Redbud is the hallmark of spring in the Sierra
Nevada foothills. The deciduous heart-shaped leaves, which emerge
after the pink blossoms, alternate on the branch. The young leaves
are bright copper-green all summer before turning reddish brown in
the autumn. In spring, small, pea-shaped flowers thickly cover the
naked branches, giving the impression of a pink cloud of color from
afar. The upper petals are smaller than the keel, which is formed by
the two lower petals. In summer, the flat, oblong fruit elongates and
dries brown. When shaken, the seeds inside the dry pod will rattle.
Western Redbud seeds need scarification to sprout; fire is the preferred method of distressing the hard seed coat, but physical scrap-
ing or boiling of the seeds may also result in successful sprouting.
Redbud grows predominately in the foothills but can also be found
in the Lower Montane environment on dry, sunny slopes. At higher
elevations, it can also be cultivated successfully if grown on warm
western exposures. Western Redbud twigs are utilized as a basketry
fiber to provide the mahogany-colored pattern in many early and
modern baskets.

Bush Lupine
Lupinus albifrons

Botanical Family: Fabaceae
Elevation: Below 6,600 ft. (2000 m)
Plant Community Zone: Sierra Nevada Foothills, Lower Montane
Shrub Height: Up to 16 ft. (5 m)
Flower: Large and violet to lavender
Fruit: Dehiscent pod that expels round, mottled seeds
Distribution: Open sandy and rocky areas

In spring, the silver-green palmate foliage of the Bush Lupine is a dramatic companion for its elongated blue flower. Small flowers bloom successively up purple stems and, while the top flowers are still blooming, the lower, pollinated blossoms develop into a pubescent peapod-like fruit. At maturity, the pod explodes with an audible pop and the tan mottled seeds are expelled a remarkable distance from the parent shrub, resulting in many seedlings the following year. The Bush Lupine is commonly found in the foothill region of the Sierra Nevada and thrives in recently disturbed areas as well as in difficult soil conditions. Nitrogen-fixing nodules on the roots of the *Fabaceae* family actually enrich the soils inhabited by the plants. As the Bush Lupine ages, it becomes rangy and open, with gray bark shedding in long strips; if it is pruned back, however, it can be a robust, compact, and attractive flowering shrub for a native plant garden.

Sierra Gooseberry
Ribes roezlii

Botanical Family: Grossulariaceae
Elevation: Below 9,200 ft. (2800 m)
Plant Community Zone: Sierra Nevada Foothills, Lower and Upper
    Montane, Subalpine
Shrub Height: Up to 7 ft. (2 m)
Flower: Pendulous, magenta and white, and with elongated repro-
    ductive parts
Fruit: Spherical, red, prickly, and edible
Distribution: Open woodlands and coniferous forests

The gooseberry family of shrubs is large and varied, and many rep-
resentative species inhabit the Sierra Nevada. The Sierra Gooseberry has numerous sharp spines along older, gray stems, and in
some cases the spines are hidden by clusters of leaves and can be
painful if the shrub is grasped or brushed against. Deciduous leaves
are grouped together atop short, gray stems that alternate along
the branch. The leaves are lobed and their margins are toothed.
Flowers of the genus *Ribes* are very showy, and Sierra Gooseberry
blooms in particular look vaguely like the familiar fuchsia flower.
The pendulous flowers are purple and white; colorful reflexed sepals
are purple, with white petals hanging downward, encircling the
exposed reproductive parts of the flower. When pollinated, the
inferior ovary swells and develops into a spherical, red, prickly fruit.
In late summer and early autumn, the fruit ripens a deep red and is
edible if one can avoid the defensive spines. Sierra Gooseberry fruit
can be made into a delicious jam, and the shrub is often cultivated
for that purpose. The Currant is a common companion plant of the
Gooseberry—found in many of the same areas—and although the
two species can look similar, the Currant is differentiated by larger
leaves, no stem spines, and small, bright red berries that grow in
dense clumps. The habitat for Sierra Gooseberry is coniferous forests and open woodlands.

Yerba Santa
Eriodictyon californicum

Botanical Family: Hydrophyllaceae
Elevation: 200–6,200 ft. (60–1900 m)
Plant Community Zone: Sierra Nevada Foothills, Lower Montane
Shrub Height: 3–10 ft. (1–3 m)
Flower: Small, funnel-shaped, and light purple
Fruit: Dark brown or black with four valves containing many
    brownish seeds
Distribution: Disturbed soils, chaparral, and arid environments

Yerba Santa is a sparse upright shrub that can be found in disturbed sandy soils along Sierra Nevada roadways. Older stems are a pale gray color, while new stems have a purple-green hue and display elongated lance-shaped leaves arranged alternately along the branch. Sticky stems and leaves give off a pleasant odor when bruised or rubbed between the fingers. The upper side of the toothed-edge leaf is a dark, glossy green and has a prominent midvein; the lower side is hairy, with a net-like pattern of small veins. Small, light purple flowers are clustered near the tops of the stems, and unopened buds have uniform, linear furrows. Fused, funnel-shaped flowers are flared open at the ends of the petals to reveal tiny, dark blue anthers. The dark brown or black fruit is small and has four valves, each containing many seeds. Preferred environments of the Yerba Santa are chaparral, open woodlands, dry slopes, and disturbed areas. There is historical evidence of medicinal usage of this adaptable shrub, and some people still use Yerba Santa medicinally. Yerba Santa translates from Spanish as "saintly" or "sacred herb."

California Rose
Rosa californica

Botanical Family: Rosaceae
Elevation: Below 5,300 ft. (1600 m)
Plant Community Zone: Sierra Nevada Foothills, Lower Montane
Shrub Height: 3–8 ft. (90 cm–2.5 m)
Flower: Pastel pink petals surround numerous yellow stamens
Fruit: Red, fleshy hypanthium (rose hip) encasing several achenes
Distribution: Shady forests and woodlands and riparian areas

California Rose is a sparsely prickled shrub that is visually interesting when in flower and in fruit. Older stems are stiff, woody, and upright and they clump together forming dense thickets. New stem growth is supple and light green in color. Thorns are generally curved and appear intermittently along the stems. The elliptic leaves are pinnate, located opposite each other along the stems, and the leaf margins are strongly toothed. Long, green sepals with pointed tips support pastel pink petals. In the center of the flower is an abundance of yellow stamens and numerous pistils. During late summer, autumn, and winter, the vibrant red fruits that hang off the ends of the branches are often referred to as "rose hips." Several achenes are encased within the fleshy, red hypanthium, which is crowned with brown or green curved sepals. The California Rose prefers habitats with water, such as riparian areas, wet meadows, or moist forests and woodlands.

Spiraea
Spiraea densiflora

Botanical Family: Rosaceae
Elevation: 2,000–11,200 ft. (600–3400 m)
Plant Community Zone: Lower and Upper Montane, Subalpine, Alpine
Shrub Height: 8 in.–3 ft. (20–90 cm)
Flower: Small, pink, bell-shaped, and with many elongated pink stamens
Fruit: Dry, brown follicles encasing numerous small seeds
Distribution: Coniferous forests, moist woodlands, and riparian areas

Spiraea is a small, delicate shrub found at the higher elevations of the Sierra Nevada. The wood of older branches is brownish, while smooth, younger branches are rose-colored. Slender, upright stems have alternating elliptic to oblanceolate leaves that are toothed near the top and smooth along the lower edges. Tight clusters of deep-pink, bell-shaped flowers sit atop thin stems. Mounded groupings of flowers have a feathery appearance on top due to the numerous pink stamens that protrude beyond the five petals. When pollinated, the flower clusters and stems become dry and brown. The fruit of the Spiraea is dry, with five follicles that encapsulate numerous small seeds. This shrub can be found with tight buds, pink flowers, and brown fruit all at the same time on one plant. Suitable habitat for Spiraea includes moist, rocky outcroppings, riparian areas, and shady coniferous forests.

Western Poison Oak
Toxicodendron diversilobum

Botanical Family: Anacardiaceae
Elevation: Below 5,400 ft. (1650 m)
Plant Community Zone: Sierra Nevada Foothills, Lower Montane
Shrub Height: 20 in.–13 ft. (50 cm–4 m)
Flower: Small, numerous, and yellowish green
Fruit: Round, leathery, and creamy white
Distribution: Chaparral, oak woodlands, open slopes, and canyons

Contact with any resinous parts of the Western Poison Oak presents the possibility of a dermatological reaction. Considered the most toxic of Sierra Nevada shrubs, Western Poison Oak is most often found in a "shrubby" form, but it can also be seen twining as a vine around trees or shrubs. Stems are a muted gray in summer but can turn reddish brown in winter. Deciduous leaves show brilliant autumn hues of red and orange. Alert hikers will easily recognize the characteristic leaf groupings: three glossy leaves forming a triad or fleur-de-lis. Numerous small, yellowish flowers are hidden under the leaves in spring and, when pollinated, present pedicels holding spherical cream-colored fruits against the red autumn foliage. Western Poison Oak is found in many habitats on the western slope of the Sierra Nevada: canyons, dry hillsides, shaded oak woodlands, and open sunny slopes are all home to this hearty shrub. When shade abounds, the plant tends to lengthen into a vine-like form, using other plants as support for its long tendrils. Skin contact with this shrub can cause severe reactions, from itchyness to weeping pustules, so hikers should be well acquainted with Western Poison Oak in all its seasonal variations.

Rubber Rabbitbrush
Chrysothamnus nauseosus

Botanical Family: Asteraceae
Elevation: 200–10,800 ft. (60–3300 m)
Plant Community Zone: Sierra Nevada Foothills, Lower and Upper
    Montane, Subalpine
Shrub Height: Up to 9 ft. (2.8 m)
Flower: Numerous, yellow, and clustered densely atop stems
Fruit: Tan or brown bristled pappus
Distribution: Dry rocky scrub, open woodlands, and sandy washes

Rubber Rabbitbrush in bloom presents an interesting contrast of texture and color. This shrub has light green stems that are punctuated with small, narrow, sessile, or stemless, leaves atop older, woody gray-brown stems. The foliage has a strong odor when bruised or crushed, and many people find the scent unpleasant. Rabbitbrush in bloom is also a common cause of respiratory allergies. The small flowers are bright yellow and clustered densely in a rounded shape on the tops of the stems. A close look shows the flowers exhibit vertically keeled bracts below the divided corolla. The stigma and style protrude beyond the corolla and look like numerous yellow hairs. In late summer or autumn, Rubber Rabbitbrush develops a unique fruit called a pappus, which appears from a distance as a grouping of stiff, fuzzy, light brown hairs. This shrub is common in diverse arid habitats and can be found in dry scrub, open woodlands, and sandy washes. Rubber Rabbitbrush and Sagebrush are often found together as companion shrubs.

Oregon Grape
Berberis aquifolium

Botanical Family: Berberidaceae
Elevation: Below 7,200 ft. (2200 m)
Plant Community Zone: Sierra Nevada Foothills, Lower and Upper
  Montane
Shrub Height: 4 in.–7 ft. (10 cm–2 m)
Flower: Small but showy, and entirely bright yellow
Fruit: Round and dark blue to purple
Distribution: Coniferous forests, woodlands, canyons, and chaparral

Oregon Grape has the appearance of holly and frequently is mistaken for something other than what it is. This stiffly erect shrub has older stems that are textured and grayish, while the new stems are smooth and reddish in color. The leaves are leathery and dark green with scalloped edges that form points, each ending with a sharp spine. Young leaves are softer and thinner, and new growth has a reddish hue. The flowers are small but numerous and densely clustered together. Sepals and petals are bright yellow and attractive against the dark evergreen leaves. When pollinated, the flowers become equally interesting fruits: dark blue to purple ovoid fruits hang close to the branches and resemble blueberries. Oregon Grape is found in a variety of environments, from coniferous forests, open woodlands, and sloped canyons to chaparral. Accidental close encounters with this plant can result in painful leaf spines penetrating the skin, and the roots of this genus have been found in some cases to be toxic. Oregon Grape is cultivated as an ornamental shrub for landscaping along freeway areas and in drought-tolerant gardens of the West.

Bush Chinquapin
Chrysolepis sempervirens

Botanical Family: Fagaceae
Elevation: 2,300–10,800 ft. (700–3300 m)
Plant Community Zone: Sierra Nevada Foothills, Lower and Upper
    Montane, Subalpine
Shrub Height: Up to 10 ft. (3 m)
Flower: Inconspicuous, yellowish-green, clustered upright, with
    both male and female flowers
Fruit: Green or brown, round, spiny burr
Distribution: Coniferous forests, open slopes, and chaparral

Bush Chinquapin is an evergreen shrub that stands out in winter
with its large, leathery leaves contrasted against the snow. Under
heavy snowfall, the flexible branches bend to the ground, rebound-
ing as the snow melts on sunny days. The main branches of the
Bush Chinquapin are covered with smooth, thin, grayish bark,
while the younger stems are light green. The blade of the leaf is
elliptical with a round to tapered tip, and the leaf edges slightly roll
under. Young leaves are covered on the underside with tiny golden
scales that to the naked eye have the appearance of a gold pubescence or fuzz. Staminate and pistillate flowers are small upright
structures located together at the ends of the branches. (Pistillate
flowers are fertile but have sterile or absent stamens; staminate
flowers are fertile but have sterile or absent pistils.) What really
captures an observer's attention, however, is the fruit of the Bush
Chinquapin. Growing solitary or in small groups, large, spiny, ovoid
burrs act as armor to guard the inner nuts from hungry animals.
Humans also should avoid grabbing the fruit; only a careful, gentle
inspection will prevent injury to the fingers from the stiff spines.
Bush Chinquapin is found in the understory of coniferous forests,
on open, rocky slopes, and in chaparral.

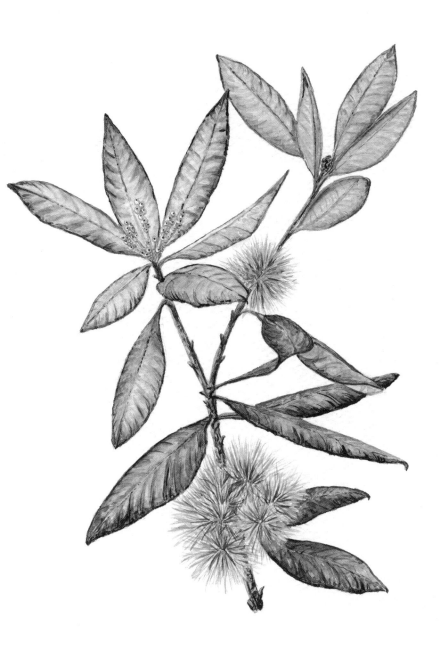

California Bay
Umbellularia californica

Botanical Family: Lauraceae
Elevation: Below 5,300 ft. (1600 m)
Plant Community Zone: Sierra Nevada Foothills, Lower Montane
Shrub Height: Up to 150 ft. (45 m)
Flower: Small, pale yellow, and clustered in upper leaves
Fruit: Large, round, and green, drying to a wrinkled brown
Distribution: Open slopes, canyons, and chaparral

A large upright shrub, the California Bay may well be one of the most aromatic plants of the Sierra Nevada. Multiple gray trunks give way to younger green stems that have large, oblong evergreen leaves. Heavily veined, glossy leaves alternate on the branch and have smooth margins. Dead, dry leaves on the forest floor emit an incredibly strong aroma when crushed underfoot, and on sunny days the oils in the leaves fill the surrounding air with a pleasant scent. The small, pale yellow flowers are clustered near the ends of the branches. What appear to be six petals is actually the calyx, which opens like petals arranged around the reproductive structures of the plant, including the nine stamens surrounding a single ovary. After pollenization, a large, yellowish green, ovoid fruit hangs dramatically from the branches. When dry, the fruit is wrinkled and dark brown. California Bay is found inhabiting canyons, open slopes, and chaparral. The leaves of this shrub can be dried and used in cooking, particularly as a flavoring for pizza, pasta sauce, hearty stews, and soups, but just as with the Turkish Bay leaves found at the grocery store, California Bay leaves should be removed from food after cooking.

Bush Poppy
Dendromecon rigida

Botanical Family: Papaveraceae
Elevation: Below 5,900 ft. (1800 m)
Plant Community Zone: Sierra Nevada Foothills, Lower Montane
Shrub Height: 3–10 ft. (1–3 m)
Flower: Large and yellow, with satiny petals
Fruit: Elongated pod that expels many smooth, brown seeds
Distribution: Sunny slopes, gravelly hillsides, and rocky canyons

Bush Poppy in bloom lights up arid ridges in the lower elevations of the western Sierra Nevada with bright yellow splashes of color. Elliptic leaves are toothed along the margins, and the undersides reveal a network of veins. Large yellow flowers sit solitary above the foliage of the Bush Poppy. The four buttery petals are soft and satiny and they drop off soon after the ovary is pollinated. Clustered around the ovary are anywhere between ten to twenty stamens. The fruit is an elongated pod that encases abundant smooth, dark brown seeds, which are ejected from the fruit as it splits open, increasing the chances of young sprouts. This drought-tolerant shrub is most at home on dry, gravelly hillsides and washes, sunny outcrops, and rocky canyon walls. Bush Poppy is also found in recently burned and disturbed areas. Despite its beauty and desirability, this native shrub is, unfortunately, difficult to grow as a permanent specimen in personal gardens, partially because it doesn't respond well to the soil amendments and general fuss that often characterize home gardens.

Bush Monkeyflower
Mimulus aurantiacus

Botanical Family: Scrophulariaceae
Elevation: Below 5,300 ft. (1600 m)
Plant Community Zone: Sierra Nevada Foothills, Lower Montane
Shrub Height: 2–4 ft. (60 cm–1.2 m)
Flower: Orange or salmon-colored, and irregularly shaped
Fruit: Dry, funnel-shaped, and with numerous seeds
Distribution: Arid environments, disturbed soils, and chaparral

In arid environments, one has a good chance of encountering the Bush Monkeyflower. This hardy shrub has thick, leathery evergreen leaves with small teeth along the margins. The leaves are arranged opposite each other on the branches but are sometimes accompanied by groups of smaller leaves. Each leaf is attached directly to the main branch, without any leaf stalk, an attachment configuration called "sessile." The leaf shape is linear to lance-like, and the leaves may be sticky to the touch. Bush Monkeyflower has beautiful, asymmetrical orange to salmon-colored flowers. Five unequal petals flare out from a tube-like base; three dissimilar lobes protrude from the bottom part of the flower, and the upper two lobes curve back exposing a white throat accented by dark orange splotches. The fruit is elongated or round, splitting open along an upper suture that reveals numerous small, egg-shaped seeds. Bush Monkeyflower prefers sunny slopes, dry hillsides, rocky ledges, disturbed areas, chaparral, and open forest and woodland. This drought-tolerant plant is sometimes utilized in native plant gardens.

Flannelbush
Fremontodendron californicum

Botanical Family: Sterculiaceae
Elevation: 1,300–6,600 ft. (400–2000 m)
Plant Community Zone: Sierra Nevada Foothills, Lower and Upper
   Montane
Shrub Height: 7–26 ft. (2–8 m)
Flower: Large and yellow, with fleshy reproductive structures
Fruit: Green, egg-shaped, hairy, and enclosed by a papery calyx
Distribution: Open forests and woodlands, exposed slopes, and
   canyons

Flannelbush is a large, many-branched shrub that grows in the foot-hill region of the western Sierra Nevada. Thick, woody, light gray branches can be seen both spreading across the ground and growing upright, sometimes nearly as tall as the shrub is wide. Atop small woody spurs are grouped thick, leathery evergreen leaves, which can be ovate, round, or lobed. The leaves have small, dense hairs on their upper and lower surfaces and can cause skin irritation on direct contact. Leaf stems can be brown or reddish in color. Soli-tary, large, yellow, bowl-shaped flowers grow among the leaves or atop their own individual woody stems. What appear at first to be petals are actually sepals; there are no petals on this flower. Five yel-low sepals are differentiated at the base by five sunken, green, hairy pits. A rigid five-pronged base in the throat of the flower supports the reproductive structures, which feature five fleshy orange sta-mens that curve away from the slender yellow pistil. The large fruit of the Flannelbush is hairy, egg-shaped, and encapsulated within the dried calyx. This striking and drought-tolerant shrub is found in dry environments, including arid woodlands, open slopes and ridges, and sometimes chaparral.

Sagebrush
Artemesia tridentata

Botanical Family: Asteraceae
Elevation: 1,000–9,800 ft. (300–3000 m)
Plant Community Zone: Sierra Nevada Foothills, Lower and Upper
    Montane, Subalpine
Shrub Height: Up to 10 ft. (3 m)
Flower: Small, gray-green, and closely aligned along an upright
    stem
Fruit: Tiny, inconspicuous glandular fruit that varies among
    subspecies
Distribution: Disturbed soils and arid environments

For many people, Sagebrush has come to represent arid western landscapes. This woody, gray-green shrub is ubiquitous in open, sandy areas. Sagebrush has grayish bark that peels in long strips from the perennial stems. Each gray-green hairy leaf is wedge-shaped and generally has three rounded teeth on the tip. Numerous small flowers are arranged amidst scarce leaves along an upright stem that is exposed above other herbaceous plant parts. The flowers are nearly monochromatic and do not appear distinct from the leaves and stems. The tiny glandular fruit develops along the stems and is inconspicuous. Sagebrush thrives on open slopes, dry gravel, and sandy washes. Most of its plant parts are intensely fragrant and, when bruised or crushed, exude a pleasant scent. Some native and local peoples use the dried stems, leaves, and flowers as incense, and burning Sagebrush has been and is presently used at some Native American tribal gatherings in rituals and ceremonies. Sagebrush plant communities have increased their dominance over large areas of the western United States; grazing, disturbed soils, and a change in local environments have perhaps contributed to an increase in the number of Sagebrush habitats.

Hazelnut
Corylus cornuta

Botanical Family: Betulaceae
Elevation: Below 6,900 ft. (2100 m)
Plant Community Zone: Sierra Nevada Foothills, Lower and Upper
  Montane
Shrub Height: Up to 13 ft. (4 m)
Flower: Female flower resembles a terminal bud; male flower is an
  elongated catkin
Fruit: Green, vase-shaped covering over an edible brown nut
Distribution: Damp, shady forests and moist woodlands

The deciduous Hazelnut can be considered either a large shrub or a
small multiple-branched tree. Younger stems are covered with soft
hairs tipped with small glands, and older branches feature large,
soft, hairy leaves in an alternating pattern. Leaf margins are highly
variable and irregularly toothed, but in autumn all the leaves turn
bright yellowish gold and the shrub stands out against the dark
green coniferous trees. The male catkins hang from the branch
tips in the early spring; the female flowers look like small, hairy
terminal buds. The fruit of the Hazelnut starts out enclosed in a
hairy, green, papery covering but matures to a delicious nut that is
highly prized by forest animals. Many people refer to the fruit of the
Hazelnut as a filbert, and one genus of this species is cultivated for
its tasty, edible nuts. This large shrub is found mostly in damp and
shady habitats but it is also adaptable enough for a variety of environments. Some native peoples still use the flexible young stems of
the Hazelnut in basketry.

Sierra Coffeeberry
Rhamnus rubra

Botanical Family: Rhamnaceae
Elevation: 3,300–7,200 ft. (1000–2200 m)
Plant Community Zone: Sierra Nevada Foothills, Lower and Upper
    Montane
Shrub Height: Up to 7 ft. (2 m)
Flower: Tiny, greenish, star-shaped, and tightly clustered
Fruit: Round, pinkish, fleshy, and ripening to a deep black color
Distribution: Open woodlands, forest scrub, and chaparral

Sierra Coffeeberry is an upright shrub known for its small, inconspicuous flowers and noticeable fruits. The young stems are green or red while the older, woody stems are mottled red and gray. Deciduous elliptic leaves can be either finely toothed or smooth on their margins. Upper leaf surfaces are a dark evergreen color; the lower surfaces are lighter green. Minute flowers grow in clusters from umbels on the ends of lateral branches. Tiny flowers are greenish and star-shaped, with flower parts growing in groups of five each (that is, five sepals and five petals). When pollinated, the flower develops into a fleshy, berry-like fruit that ripens from a pinkish yellow to a deep black that is a striking contrast with the yellowing leaves of autumn. The diversity within the *Rhamnus* genus can make it difficult to distinguish between recognized varieties; the Sierra Coffeeberry is sometimes mistaken for the California Coffeeberry, *Rhamnus californica*, which is evergreen instead of deciduous. The Sierra Coffeeberry is found in a wide range of habitats that includes open woodlands, forest scrub, sagebrush communities, and chaparral slopes.

Birch-leaf Mountain Mahogany
Cercocarpus betuloides

Botanical Family: Rosaceae
Elevation: Below 8,200 ft. (2500 m)
Plant Community Zone: Sierra Nevada Foothills, Lower and Upper
  Montane
Shrub Height: 7–26 ft. (2–8 m)
Flower: Green, funnel-shaped, and with numerous protruding
  stamens
Fruit: Brown, feathery, spiraled plume atop a hairy seed
Distribution: Coniferous forests, open slopes, and chaparral

Birch-leaf Mountain Mahogany may not look like a typical rose,
but it shares characteristics with other species in the family Rosaceae. This large shrub has numerous gray branches that grow and
spread upward. Many small leaves are clustered together atop small
stems that alternate along the main branches. Leaves are laterally
veined, with the upper leaf surfaces a deep green and the lower leaf
surfaces a pale green between the darker leaf veins. The leaves are
fan-shaped, narrowing near the stem and broadening into a wedge
near the tip. Abundant small flowers grow in groups among the
leaves. The flowers do not have petals, but the other flower parts
are held together by a flared, green, funnel-shaped hypanthium. A
plethora of stamens line the flower's perimeter and arch back over
the hypanthium, giving the flowers a hairy appearance. The anthers
are tan and hairy. In late summer or autumn, the fruit of the Birch-
leaf Mountain Mahogany emerges, and each hairy, one-chambered
structure displays a long, feathery, spiraled plume or tail; the genus
name *Cercocarpus* is a combination of the Greek words for "tail"
and "fruit." This unique form of the fruit aids in its dispersal as it
is easily carried by the wind and often catches in the fur of passing
wildlife. Birch-leaf Mountain Mahogany is typically found in coniferous forests, open slopes, chaparral, and dry habitats.

Lemmon's Willow
Salix lemmonii

Botanical Family: Salicaceae
Elevation: 4,600–11,500 ft. (1400–3500 m)
Plant Community Zone: Lower and Upper Montane, Subalpine, Alpine
Shrub Height: Up to 13 ft. (4 m)
Flower: Dense, tan, silky catkins, with male and female flowers growing on separate plants
Fruit: Bivalved
Distribution: Subalpine forests, meadows, and riparian areas

It can be difficult to differentiate species of willows. In some cases, without fresh specimens, a dissecting microscope, and a good plant key, it may be nearly impossible to identify a particular species. As a generalized group, however, willows are more readily distinguished from other plants: fast-growing, thickly branched shrubs or dense trees with roots near water and long, slender leaves are usually willows. Lemmon's Willow is shrubby, with brownish older branches and supple, light green younger stems and leaves. The leaf shape is elliptic to lance-like with smooth leaf margins. The upper leaf surfaces are shiny and darker green while the lower surfaces are gray-green and silky with hairs. Lemmon's Willow is a dioecious shrub, meaning that individual plants produce either male (staminate) or female (pistillate) reproductive flower parts but never both on the same shrub. Dense catkins form on both male and female plants at the same time as the young leaves, and from there one of two things happens: (1) staminate flowers display numerous tan stamens protruding beyond the body of the catkin or (2) pistillate flowers, when pollinated, become silky, ivory-colored catkins. Lemmon's Willows, like other willows, prefer their roots near water, whether marshlands, streams, or moist meadows. Supple willow twigs are frequently utilized in basketry.

Glossary of Terms

achene. Dry, one-seeded fruit.

aggregate. Structure to which flower parts or aggregate fruits are attached.

anther. Pollen end of the stamen.

axil. Angle between a leaf and its stem.

calyx. Collective term for sepals that subtend the petals.

capsule. Dry, many-seeded fruit.

catkin. Spike of unisexual flowers usually hanging downward.

corolla. Collective term for petals.

dehiscent. Describing a mature fruit that splits to release its seeds.

dioecious. Describing species on which male and female flowers grow on separate plants.

disturbed area. An environment that has been manipulated or changed by a natural or human-induced event, such as a fire.

drupe. Fleshy, smooth-skinned fruit that encases a stony seed, as in a cherry or plum.

entire. Describing leaf margins that are smooth.

filament. Stalk holding up the anther.

glandular. Bearing surface glands, which often exude a sticky substance.

glaucous. White, powdery, or waxy in appearance.

hand lens. Small magnifying lens utilized in the field to observe minute details.

herbaceous. Having soft, not woody, plant tissue.

hypanthium. Fused lower portion of flower parts.

inflorescence. Cluster of flowers in its entirety.

keel. Center ridge or crease; in the *Fabacea* family the keel is made up of the two lower petals.

leaf out. The process of bright green leaves unfurling in spring before the flowers open.

lobe. Large projection on the edge of a leaf or a flower part.

midvein. Dominant center vein, usually on a leaf.

oblanceolate. Describing an oval-shaped leaf that tapers toward the stem.

ovary. Enlarged part of the pistil that contains ovules.

ovate. Describing a leaf shaped like an egg.

ovule. Female part of the flower that contains an unfertilized egg.

palmate. Having leaf parts (e.g., lobes, leaflets, or veins) radiating from a central point.

pappus. Group of structures (usually hairs, bristles, or scales) at the top of an *Asteraceae* ovary.

pedicel. Stalk holding up a flower or fruit.

petal. Individual member of the corolla, often known for its color.

petiole. Stalk that attaches a leaf to a branch.

pinnate. Shaped like a feather.

pistil. Female reproductive structure of a flower.

pistillate. Having fertile pistils.

pubescence. Covering of soft, short hairs.

raceme. Inflorescence of flowers attached by short stalks to a central stem and that bloom from bottom to top.

receptacle. The portion of the flower stalk where the flower parts or flower heads are attached.

reflexed. Curved backward.

resinous. Describing plants or trees that exude a viscous, translucent organic substance, such as sap.

riparian. Along the side of a river or other small body of water.

root-sprout. Process of new leaves emerging from an existing root clump, particularly after a fire.

scarification. Scratching the seed surface to encourage germination.

sepal. Individual part of the outer whorl of the calyx, and usually green in color.

serrate. Describing leaf margins with sharp teeth.

sessile. Describing a leaf without a supporting stalk.

shrubby. Describing a woody, perennial plant that has many basal branches and is smaller than a tree.

spike. Unbranched stem of sessile flowers.

spur. Hollow extension that extends from a flower and usually contains nectar.

stamen. Male reproductive structure of a flower.

staminate. Having fertile stamens.

stigma. Generally sticky female receptacle for pollen.

style. Thin stalk that connects an ovary to a stigma.

subtend. To be situated closely beneath, as in the position of sepals relative to petals.

suture. Seam of union; line of fusion.

umbel. Many flower pedicels fanning out from a common point.

valve. One of the parts into which a capsule splits.

venation. Pattern of leaf veins.

xeric. Adapted to arid habitats.

KEY TO FLOWER AND LEAF MORPHOLOGY

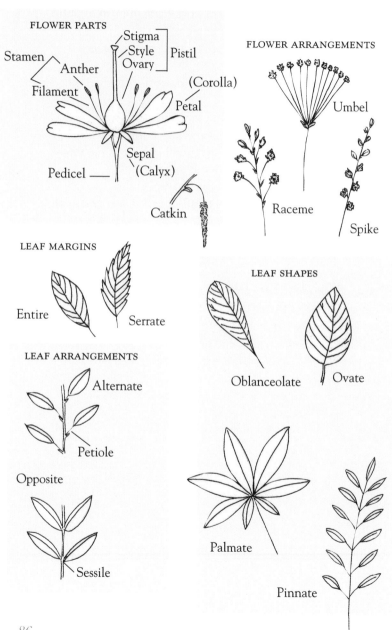

FLOWER PARTS

Stigma
Style — Pistil
Ovary

Stamen
Anther
Filament

(Corolla)
Petal

Sepal
(Calyx)

Pedicel

Catkin

FLOWER ARRANGEMENTS

Umbel

Raceme

Spike

LEAF MARGINS

Entire

Serrate

LEAF SHAPES

Oblanceolate

Ovate

LEAF ARRANGEMENTS

Alternate

Petiole

Opposite

Sessile

Palmate

Pinnate

Distribution Areas

Sierra Nevada Foothills: Bordering the Central Valley on the west side of the Sierra Nevada. A land of hot, dry summers with little or no snow in the winter. Mixed woodland interspersed with extensive grasslands. Example: El Portal.

Lower Montane: Located between the Sierra Nevada Foothills and the Upper Montane areas. A land of warm, dry summers with rain and snow during the winter. Large and diverse mix of conifers and deciduous trees. Example: Yosemite Valley.

Upper Montane: Located between the Lower Montane and the Subalpine regions. A land of short, cool, and moist summers and cold and snowy winters. Huge evergreens dominate the forest. Example: Glacier Point Road.

Subalpine: Located between the Upper Montane forests and the Alpine regions. A land of cool summers and long, cold, and exceptionally snowy winters. Located just below the treeline. Example: Tuolumne Meadows.

Alpine: Located above the Subalpine region and the treeline. A land of short, cool summers with long, cold, and snowy winters. Sparse floral coverage and a high degree of exposure to the elements. Example: Tioga Pass.

References

Blackwell, L. R. (1999). *Wildflowers of the Sierra Nevada and the Central Valley*. Renton, WA: Lone Pine Publishing.

Bowers, J. E. (1993). *Shrubs and Trees of the Southwest Deserts*. Tuscon: Southwest Parks and Monuments Association.

Elmore, F. H. (1976). *Shrubs and Trees of the Southwest Uplands*. Tuscon: Southwest Parks and Monuments Association.

Gerstenberg, R. H. (1983). *Common Trees and Shrubs of the Southern Sierra Nevada*. Self-published.

Hickman, J. C. (1993). *The Jepson Manual: Higher Plants of California*. Berkeley: University of California Press.

Lanner, R. M. (1999). *Conifers of California*. Los Olivos, CA: Cachuma Press.

Morgenson, D. C. (1975). *Yosemite Wildflower Trails*. El Portal, CA: Yosemite Association.

Pavlik, B. M., P. C. Muick, S. G. Johnson, and M. Popper. (2000). *Oaks of California*. Los Olivos, CA: Cachuma Press.

Storer, T. I., and R. L. Usinger. (1963). *Sierra Nevada Natural History*. Berkeley: University of California Press.

Stuart, J. D., and J. O. Sawyer. (2001). *Trees and Shrubs of California*. Berkeley: University of California Press.

Thomas, J. H. (1974). *Native Shrubs of the Sierra Nevada*. Berkeley: University of California Press.

Whitney, S. (1979). *A Sierra Club Naturalist's Guide to the Sierra Nevada*. San Francisco: Sierra Club Books.

——— (1982). *A Field Guide to the Grand Canyon*. New York: William Morrow and Company, Inc.

Wilson, L., J. Wilson, and J. Nicholas. (1987). *Wildflowers of Yosemite*. El Portal, CA: Sierra Press, Inc.

Common Name Index

American Dogwood, 4
Birch-leaf Mountain
    Mahogany, 78
Bitter Cherry, 34
Blue Elderberry, 2
Bush Chinquapin, 62
Bush Lupine, 46
Bush Monkeyflower, 68
Bush Poppy, 66
California Bay, 64
California Buckeye, 18
California Rose, 52
Chamise, 28
Deer Brush, 26
Flannelbush, 70
Greenleaf Manzanita, 8
Hazelnut, 74
Huckleberry Oak, 16
Lemmon's Willow, 80
Mock Orange, 22
Mountain Heather, 42
Mountain Misery, 30
Mountain Whitethorn, 24
Oregon Grape, 60
Pinemat Manzanita, 6

Rubber Rabbitbrush, 58
Sagebrush, 72
Sierra Coffeeberry, 76
Sierra Gooseberry, 48
Snowberry, 40
Spicebush, 38
Spiraea, 54
Thimbleberry, 36
Toyon, 32
Tree Anemone, 20
Western Azalea, 14
Western Poison Oak, 56
Western Redbud, 44
White Heather, 12
Whiteleaf Manzanita, 10
Yerba Santa, 50

Scientific Name Index

Adenostoma fasciculatum, 28
Aesculus californica, 18
Arctostaphylos nevadensis, 6
Arctostaphylos patula, 8
Arctostaphylos viscida, 10
Artemisia tridentata, 72
Berberis aquifolium, 60
Calycanthus occidentalis, 38
Carpenteria californica, 20
Cassiope mertensiana, 12
Ceanothus cordulatus, 24
Ceanothus integerrimus, 26
Cercis occidentalis, 44
Cercocarpus betuloides, 78
Chamaebatia foliolosa, 30
Chrysolepis sempervirens, 62
Chrysothamnus nauseosus, 58
Cornus sericea, 4
Corylus cornuta, 74
Dendromecon rigida, 66
Eriodictyon californicum, 50
Fremontodendron
    californicum, 70
Heteromeles arbutifolia, 32
Lupinus albifrons, 46

Mimulus aurantiacus, 68
Philadelphus lewisii, 22
Phyllodoce breweri, 42
Prunus emarginata, 34
Quercus vaccinifolia, 16
Rhamnus rubra, 76
Rhododendron occidentale, 14
Ribes roezlii, 48
Rosa californica, 52
Rubus parviflorus, 36
Salix lemmonii, 80
Sambucus mexicana, 2
Spiraea densiflora, 54
Symphoricarpos albus, 40
Toxicodendron diversilobum, 56
Umbellularia californica, 64

Artist's Note

I HAVE BEEN creating art since I was a small girl. The variety of mediums I have experimented with includes chalk and oil pastel, pen and ink, charcoal, scratchboard, oil, acrylic, and watercolor. Primarily my art interests have been in rendering wilderness landscapes and botanicals utilizing watercolor. Art is the way I express my love for the natural world. The intricacy of a flower petal, the delicate rainbow spectrum in waterfall spray, and powerful shafts of light illuminating rugged mountain scenery all contribute to my appreciation of and enchantment with nature. It is my hope that you enjoy these watercolor paintings, created with attention to botanical accuracy and fine detail. They represent a piece of my heart and soul.

Shirley Spencer

About the Author

SHIRLEY SPENCER has lived and worked in the Sierra Nevada since 1979. She earned a B.A. in Life Science from Pacific Union College and an M.A. in Environmental Studies from Fresno Pacific University. Shirley began teaching natural history and park interpretation classes for the Yosemite Institute in 1986. In addition to teaching in Yosemite National Park, Shirley leads classes in Sequoia and Kings Canyon National Parks and she has also instructed natural history courses in Canyonlands National Park, Arches National Park, Joshua Tree National Park, and Pinnacles National Monument. Shirley is an accomplished artist specializing in watercolors, with an emphasis on Sierra Nevada landscapes and botanical illustrations. She has co-authored and published two books and several magazine articles with her husband, Mark.

The Yosemite Association is a 501(c)(3) nonprofit membership organization; since 1923, it has initiated and supported a variety of interpretive, educational, research, scientific, and environmental programs in Yosemite National Park, in cooperation with the National Park Service. Revenue generated by its publishing program, park visitor center bookstores, Yosemite Outdoor Adventures, membership dues, and donations enables it to provide services and direct financial support that promote park stewardship and enrich the visitor experience. To learn more about the association's activities and other publications, or for information about membership, please write to the Yosemite Association, P.O. Box 230, El Portal, CA 95318, call (209) 379-2646, or visit www.yosemite.org.

Heyday Books, founded in 1974, works to deepen people's understanding and appreciation of the cultural, artistic, historic, and natural resources of California and the American West. It operates under a 501(c)(3) nonprofit educational organization (Heyday Institute) and, in addition to publishing books, sponsors a wide range of programs, outreach, and events. For more information about this or about becoming a Friend of Heyday, please visit our website at www.heydaybooks.com.